TONY HAWK

ALSO BY TONY HAWK

Hawk, Occupation: Skateboarder
Between Boardslides and Burnout: My Life on the Road

TONY HAWK
PROFESSIONAL SKATEBOARDER

itbooks
AN IMPRINT OF HARPERCOLLINS PUBLISHERS

TONY HAWK
WITH SEAN MORTIMER

CONTENTS

RO

It wasn't always cool to be a skateboarder. Today, if you wear skate shoes and baggy pants, you look like most of the youth population. It's the "in" look. People of every age all over the world play skateboarding video games and know the name of complex skate tricks. If you turn on the TV there's a good chance you'll see skateboarding in a commercial or a contest. But back in the late '70s, when I started, skating was on its way out.

By the time I was obsessed with skateboarding, it was a geeky fad that only weirdos and nerds continued to do—at least that's what my schoolmates told me. I was used to hearing their taunts, though. I was twelve years old, and I was the only skater in my school. I didn't look like anybody else. Scabs covered my knees and elbows, and my clothes were ripped because I was always falling while trying new tricks. Everybody else in school had Nikes or Adidas, and I had blue high-top Vans or Converse Chuck Taylors with gray duct tape crisscrossing the toe. I had to tape them together because they were falling apart from kneesliding. My days at school were spent keeping my head down, doing my schoolwork, and counting the seconds until the final bell rang, signifying freedom. That bell allowed me to go to the local skatepark, Del Mar Skate Ranch, and skate until closing.

The days and nights spent at the skatepark saved me. All my problems—my lack of skate friends who lived close by, my tiny size, the fact that I was a walking scab collection—evaporated once I walked through the entrance door to the skatepark. I worked out any problem by skating.

Skating also taught me the meaning of focus and perseverance. One time at Del Mar when I was trying to learn a new trick, I set it up with an easy trick called a 50-50. It was simple; I just needed to grind both my trucks on the edge of the concrete bowl. I had done it thousands of times before. I could do it in my sleep. This time, though, I got stuck on the edge and started to fall. I put my hands in front of my face to protect it, but unfortunately, it was too late. My face bounced off the concrete. My mouth was full of blood.

Dazed, I stood up, and walked to the manager's office. My legs wobbled, and I couldn't walk in a straight line due to my semi-conscious state. My mouth felt weird, and when I ran my tongue

Fakie thruster at Del Mar, 1981.

against my front teeth, a bolt of pain blasted through my head. I wanted to start crying—the pain was that bad. I had broken my front teeth in half. Both were now nubs, half their original height, and sensitive, exposed nerves dangled from the end of each. My parents, who had grown used to the occasional skatepark emergency calls, picked me up and drove me to a dentist, who capped my teeth. A few months later I was goofing around in a mellow part of Del Mar, and I slammed on my face again. This time I knocked my front teeth out entirely. Like the old saying goes, if at first you don't succeed, try, try again.

Slamming didn't bother me, because I knew that was the price I had to sometimes pay to learn a new trick. And when I finally landed it, I knew it was all worth it. Afterward, I'd immediately push myself to learn a harder trick. My time spent on a skateboard built up my confidence. It didn't bother me that I didn't have a girlfriend or wasn't the popular guy at school. All I cared about was rolling around with other skaters at the park and having fun. And as far as skating goes, not much has changed since then.

1: MANIAC KID

I was an accident. My mom laughs and shakes her head no whenever I say that, but it's the truth. She prefers to say I was a surprise. My parents, who were both in their forties when I came along, thought they'd finished raising kids. When my mom had me, she was in the middle of completing her college education and my dad worked as a salesman. My oldest sister, Lenore, was off at college, my other sister, Patricia, had just graduated from high school, and Steve, my brother, was twelve years old when I, the screaming baby wrapped in a blue blanket, came home.

I was an absolute nightmare for the first decade of my life. I began committing offenses when I was still in my crib and barely able to walk, but I never felt anything but love from my family.

Because my dad worked full-time and my mom was at school, they hired an elderly, sweet nanny to watch me. I knew she loved me, but I didn't like the fact that she had control over when I ate, slept, and played. One of my earliest memories is of trying to score a direct hit on her using any toy within my hand's reach. I'd often wake up in my crib just in time to spot her peering in on me. Whenever I saw her head of willowy white, I'd grab the nearest toy and launch it at her. I rarely succeeded in hitting her, but my trying was enough to make her quit.

I tortured a list of nannies and treated some better than others. But I treated my parents worst of all. My mom has dozens of embarrassing stories of me and my spastic temper. Once, when she told me I was old enough to sleep in my own bed, in my own room, I thought differently and decided to take matters into my own hands. When I thought my parents were asleep, I began the first stage of my special operations mission. I got on my hands and knees and crawled below my parents' line of sight, or so I thought. I slinked down the hallway like a worm. Slowly and somewhat quietly, I pushed open the door to their room. Staying low, I silently crept to the edge of the bed, ready to crawl up quietly and sneak in under the covers. When I looked up to start my climb, Mom was there staring me down. I shook my fists at her, knowing my plan had been foiled. As I crawled back to my room, I swore in my mind to extract revenge at a later date.

Another time soon after, my parents sent me to bed early— probably so that they could get some well-deserved, relaxing time to themselves. I was so annoyed that I had to go to sleep while they were still up having fun, that I yanked all the sheets, pillows, and blankets off my bed. Carrying everything down the hall, I sat on the stairs and one by one threw everything at them. A shower of bedding rained down on them while they watched TV and just pretended not to notice.

My parents had to stop having guests over, because they couldn't predict how I would act. One time when I was about five years old, they thought I'd mellowed enough to invite some friends over. I ended up crawling on the table and upsetting the place settings, not to mention my parents. Needless to say, after that they didn't have any guests over for years.

No matter what I did, my parents still showered me with love. They were incapable of being disappointed with me. One of my parents' friends summed it up best when she told my mom she thought I was spoiled rotten.

"He's not spoiled rotten," my mom replied, "he's loved."

"Well, then he's loved rotten," the friend said.

THE GREAT ESCAPE

From the time I was two, I knew I had my parents wrapped around my finger. There weren't a lot of problems I couldn't solve with a massive temper tantrum. After a while, my parents always caved in to my demands. Naturally, I thought the whole world would be as easy to manipulate.

Cold hard reality smacked me in the face moments after my dad dropped me off at Christopher Robin Preschool. I was three and short for my age. I stared up at the tall chain-link fences that surrounded the school. They seemed as high as skyscrapers—impossible to climb over to escape. I couldn't believe my parents would leave me in such a horrible place! The first day was the worst of my young life. Every day we had to run through a fire drill. We'd file outside and silently wait for instructions from the teachers. At lunchtime we were forced to sit with our head in our hands and keep silent for a minute before we ate. At that point, I don't think I'd ever maintained a full minute of silence.

The absolute worst torture the school inflicted on me was the forced nap time. I was hyper, to say the least, and I had to be running around, tapping my feet, or deeply involved in an activity or else I went bananas from boredom. I still have nightmares about trying to stay still on my sleep mat, squeezing my eyes shut as the teacher walked around checking on us. I never once fell asleep.

My terror of preschool became so great that one time my sister Lenore visited me at school and I grabbed her leg like a drowning person and wouldn't let go. I had to be pried off.

I knew I needed to get away from there, so after a few months

I became obsessed with escaping. I devised a plan. I would cry. It wasn't rocket science or anything, but it worked with my parents, so I figured it would work with my teachers, too.

The next day, after my dad dropped me off, I ran to the fence and locked my fingers onto it as tightly as I could. I shook the fence and started bawling. I'm not talking little weepy tears; snot was bubbling out of my nose, my eyes turned red, and my head whipped from side to side to ward off any teacher who tried to get close. Eventually, a few teachers would pull me away, but the next day I repeated the process.

After a few weeks of this, my dad was called into the office. Half an hour later he picked me up from class, and we drove home. I had done it! I had beaten the dreaded preschool in a test of wills. They had informed Dad that I was formally expelled. My dad thought it was funny. Instead of punishing me, he bought me an electric red toy car that I could sit in and drive, even though we couldn't really afford it. My mom says she watched me from the kitchen, zooming around, smacking into furniture with the biggest smile on my face. She commented to my dad, "Just what the world needs, another dropout with a slick car."

Sanoland, short for sanitation land. I could skate this sanitation ditch from school all the way home. Cardiff, 1983.

2: SPAZ, THAT'S ME!

When I think back on all the terrible things I did to my parents, I don't know why they put up with me. One time when my mom couldn't find a baby-sitter and had to register for college classes, she was forced to take me along with her. We had to wait in line for half an hour. My mom refused to let me run around and pillage the college campus on my own. She held my hand tight, so I couldn't escape. I became so mad that I began kicking her in the shins. I didn't stop until we had left. She was forced to register later.

I'm not proud of my attitude as a child. Now, I understand that part of my problem was my diet. My parents usually let me eat what I wanted. They had little choice—I would throw a temper tantrum if I didn't get it. Not a little angry fit; these were atomic bombs of tantrums. I freaked out so much that my mom finally let me have my own shopping cart when we went to the grocery store. I filled it with junk food. I ate sugar-coated cereals and ice cream every day. I drank more Coke than water. All the sugar and caffeine cranked me up into a frenzy, and once it mixed with my overachieving determination, I could barely control myself.

It didn't get much better when we would eat in a restaurant, which due to my behavior wasn't often. I'd order the largest meal and milk shake on the menu. My dad would lean over and warn me that if I drank the entire milk shake, I'd be too full to eat a balanced meal. I'd throw a tantrum, get the milk shake, and suck it down before our food came—and always, without fail, I'd be too full to eat anything. It got so bad that my mom stopped ordering and ate my leftovers. She always had a complete meal.

DETERMINATION

I had an overactive sense of determination, which exploded whenever I was involved in anything competitive. If I was playing a video game like Pac-Man with my brother and lost, I would throw a spaz. If I thought I was losing at checkers, I'd flip the board up, spraying checkers all over the room. If somebody had something I wanted, such as a Frisbee, I'd have to have it. If there were three or four people with Frisbees, it wasn't enough that they shared one with me—I had to have them all! I was a brat of Godzilla proportions.

When I was five, my mom thought it would be a neat idea to teach me to play tennis. She explained the rules and gently lobbed a fuzzy green ball over the net to me. I charged forward, wound my arm up like a slingshot, and hammered the ball as hard as I could directly at her. The ball blasted from my racquet and scored a direct hit on her. She laughed and told me to calm down. (She later told me that watching me run as fast as my little legs could propel me almost gave her a laughing fit.) But without fail, every ball I smacked shot over the net like a missile and either ricocheted off my mom or missed her by a mile. She stopped after a few hits and called me over.

"Now, Tony," she said with a smile, "I think you're trying to hit me on purpose."

I was so hyper that I jumped back and forth on my feet like a tap dancer.

"If you don't want to play nice, I'll stop playing and go home," she said.

I stopped thinking about blasting more balls. I didn't even

really want to play anymore. What was the point of playing a game if you didn't try to demolish your opponent?

My mom says she and my dad put up with all my cruddy attitude because they felt sorry for me. She realized I was a lot harder on myself than I was on them. She saw all the goals I set and my days spent trying to meet them. My parents were smart enough to realize that if they tried to interfere, it would frustrate me more. If my parents hadn't supported my determination, I doubt I would ever have been a sponsored skateboarder, never mind a successful professional.

GIFTED?

Even though I was a preschool bad boy, I actually enjoyed school once I was free of nap time. By second grade, I wanted to be a math teacher. Like most of my other obsessions, it had to happen right away! I couldn't wait twenty years until I finished school.

I recruited my friends from the neighborhood to meet at my house after school. I spent half an hour setting up the patio furniture in the backyard. I lined all the chairs up next to the tables and put a piece of paper with a pencil on each chair. When my "students" came, I conducted math class. I showed them how to solve problems and then walked chair-to-chair helping them if they needed it. It only lasted a few days. They didn't seem to enjoy class as much as the instructor did.

In elementary school, I learned how far to push the limits without being annoying. I was pretty mellow—almost shy. But I couldn't control my boredom and constant need to fidget. The teacher would give a lesson and I'd tap my feet, flip my pencil around on the desk, look out the window—anything to keep myself amused. The weird part was that I got high grades and understood what the teacher was saying, but every day seconds stretched into minutes and minutes seemed like hours.

My mom knew I was a hyper kid but couldn't understand why I had trouble paying attention in class. She knew I wasn't dumb. I had learned to read, write, and count before I started school from watching *Sesame Street*. She thought my problem might be that I was understimulated.

She arranged for an IQ test, and when the results came back, we found out that I had scored a 144. This was higher than the average score and it put me in the "gifted" category. The person who administered the test explained that the cause of my frustration was that my brain was constantly telling my body to do things it couldn't physically do. Because of this, I burned myself out trying to accomplish my goals and was usually disappointed with myself when I didn't meet them. So I took out my frustration on my family.

My parents had a few options. They could bump me up a grade, but they figured that starting a class with kids a year older would make me even more of a nightmare. Or, they could wait until I entered third grade and bump me up to fourth-grade reading and math.

Any ideas I had about continuing my fidgeting in the fourth-grade class were demolished my first day in reading class. The teacher whacked a smart-alecky student over the head with a pile of papers. In my third-grade mind, I figured that this was the punishment you received if you read incorrectly. When I saw it happen, I froze, my eyes bugged out, and I was scared to move and make the teacher notice me. I was positive she would give me a thrashing for being too much of a spaz.

I convinced my parents and third-grade teacher that I wasn't ready for anything as "advanced" as fourth-grade classes, and went back to trying to stay still in third-grade reading and math.

3: THE BEGINNING

By the time I was nine years old my brother and sisters had all moved out. I was especially close to my brother, Steve, who took my temper tantrums and spaz-outs in stride. When he hung out with his older buddies, he included me in a lot of their activities. We shared the same absurd sense of humor. He'd drop his towel and moon me in the hallway. He was my best friend, and when he moved to a college that was a four-hour drive away, I was devastated. But at least he'd visit once a month.

One day we were digging in the garage looking for something to do when Steve pulled out a dusty, blue fiberglass skateboard. It was almost half the width of today's boards and inches shorter. The wheels were tiny and the bearings rattled around from years of not being used.

"Try this," Steve said, and we went into the alley behind our house where there was a flat road with no cars. Because he was a surf freak, he naturally skateboarded.

From the mid-1950s up to the '70s, skateboarding was mainly an activity that surfers did when the waves were flat. They would ride supersketchy skateboards. In the beginning, a lot of them were handmade from cut-up rollerskates nailed to a piece of wood. In the '50s the wheels were made of steel. Imagine riding on a board with wheels that could be dented if you ran over a rock! Soon skaters began riding clay wheels. These were a little better, but they would eject the skater into the air if he hit a tiny rock or a crack in the sidewalk. Clay wheels also cracked over time and fell apart. The bearings used were loose and would often spill out, stopping the skateboard in an instant.

In the '70s skaters started using urethane instead of clay and the modern wheel was created. At first skaters used to do weird tricks like handstands and ballet routines on their boards. But a group of rowdy kids in Santa Monica called the Z-Boys (because they rode for a skate shop called Zephyr) forever changed the way people would skate. They never did the gymnastic type of skating; they copied what surfers were doing. They brought their distinct style to empty backyard pools, which sparked the start of vertical skating as we know it today. The main stars at the time were Tony Alva, Stacy Peralta (who would later help shape my career), and Jay Adams.

My brother was never a serious skater. He did it casually for a few years and then shoved his skateboard in the back of the garage. But he knew enough to show me how to stand and push properly. The only problem was that I couldn't turn! I pushed and drifted toward the end of the alley and either slammed into it or jumped off as my board rolled into the fence. Naturally, I whined, so Steve showed me how to turn to avoid smashing into things.

I had a good time skating that day, but to me it was the same as playing miniature golf or throwing a Frisbee around—fun, but nothing I craved doing nonstop.

About every other week I'd pull the skinny blue board out when I was bored, and would roll around in the alley by myself. Gradually, I began skating more and more. It was still nothing serious, but six months later I was skating a few times a week.

Bony Hawk. This pipe wasn't quite skateable, even for a twig like me.

A layback air. There was no chance I'd get skin cancer in the early '80s with this much skin covered.

4: JOINING THE ANTS

There were a few kids in my neighborhood who skated on a casual basis. Once or twice a week we'd gather and push around on our boards and try to improve our balance. We rarely did anything besides roll up and down the flat street.

I lived in San Diego at the time, and about twenty minutes away from my house was Oasis Skatepark, which was located under the freeway overpass. Even before my brother introduced me to skating, I would scramble to the side of the car and watch the skaters below as we drove past. They were small, like ants, and the park was full of them crisscrossing by one another at high speeds as they rode through the park. I was always amazed that they never crashed into one another—at least not that I ever saw. It looked fun, but it was a world I wasn't a part of yet.

Once I started skating more often, I begged my parents to take me to Oasis. They didn't have any extra money to waste on a skatepark membership, which they knew I would never use if I didn't enjoy it. So my dad did the next best thing—he built a slant ramp in our driveway.

If there's one thing my parents are masters at, it's encouraging their kids to follow their dreams. Before Steve had his driver's license, my dad woke up every morning as the sun came up to drive him to the beach to surf before school. My dad never complained and seemed to love it. My sister, Patricia, was in a band, and my dad built her stage sets and managed the band.

My dad had a variety of jobs throughout his life. He was a pilot during World War II and the Korean War. Later, he worked as a salesman for everything from musical instruments to *Star Wars* coffee cups. He had a bit of a problem holding on to a job, because he rarely got along with bosses. Looking back, I realize he considered it his job to encourage his kids to believe they could accomplish anything, as long as they were willing to put the hard work into it. My mom was just as positive.

After a few years of my dad's unpredictable jobs, my mom started teaching and became the breadwinner of the family. If I had had different parents, I wouldn't be nearly as successful in my life. Once they saw that I enjoyed skating the driveway ramp on an old blue board, they bought me a better one that was more modern and wider with better trucks and wheels.

EXTREME PAD WEARING

In fifth grade I got the surprise of my life when a neighborhood kid asked if I wanted to go skate Oasis with him and a few other skaters. He said his mom was going to drive a van full of his friends down on the following Saturday. I begged, and whined, and explained to my parents how horrible my life would be if they didn't let me go. They finally agreed after days of my nagging. Even though my temper had improved slightly, I was still a brat of King Kong proportions. The only difference was that by the time I was in fifth grade, my parents had become a little better at dealing with my hyper energy.

The first time I entered Oasis, I had to stop in order to take it all in. What seemed like hundreds of skaters were whipping around doing tricks on skateboards that I thought were impossible. Everybody, from older men with mustaches to young girls, was skating.

I'll never forget the blast of excitement I felt as I walked into the cluttered mobile home that Oasis Skatepark used as an office. I was finally going to be one of the tiny ants I had seen zipping around from the freeway above. People would actually look down and see *me* skating, and think I was a *real* skateboarder. I filled out the forms they gave me, was given a day pass, and told I needed to rent safety equipment.

My helmet was massive! It slid around on my head like I was wearing a bucket instead of a piece of safety equipment. The foam insert was damp and smelled like somebody else's mixture of sweat and shampoo. When I fastened my elbow pads, it felt like I was strapping cold slugs to my arms. I could almost see the germs moving around on them. I've done a lot of things in my life that some people consider dangerous. I've busted my teeth out many times, knocked myself unconscious a few more times, and broken some bones, but looking back, the most dangerous and brave "stunt" I ever did was to put on rental safety equipment.

Imagine going into a locker room immediately after a football game and putting on sweaty and dirty clothes that smelled like they were rinsed in the sewer—that's what putting on rental skate pads and helmets felt like. The normally soft elastic backing of the pads was so crusted with skaters' sweat that it hardened and made crunching sounds when it moved. White, crystallized salt coated the outside of the pads. If I was lucky I'd get one "fresher" kneepad, meaning that it was still damp from a previous user's sweat but at least the elastic didn't crunch. Still, I would have skated in my underwear if that was the rule. Once I walked through the entrance to Oasis, I didn't care what my equipment smelled like or how gross it felt. Luckily, once I got into skating, the first thing my parents invested in was my own safety gear.

I spent most of my first day at Oasis trying not to get run over. I practiced in a small, mellow beginner's bowl that was about as high as a curb. Then I tried to skate everything else in the park when it wasn't too crowded. I didn't stop the whole day.

During the ride home, I could tell something weird had happened. I felt different than I had in the morning. My mind was filling up with all the excitement from the skatepark. I wanted to learn so many different tricks! I realized later that for the first time I was feeling content. Even though I wasn't close to being a good skater, I felt happy thinking about all the possibilities skating had to offer. I wasn't frustrated or discouraged. That night all I thought about was what it must feel like to be able to skateboard like some of the experts at Oasis. I couldn't wait to go back again.

From that day on, my life changed, and my energy was spent trying to hook up rides to Oasis. My brother had finished school and moved back to San Diego to work for a newspaper. He had his own apartment, but once a week he'd drive me to Oasis and watch me skate. After a few months of chauffeuring me around, he became too busy at work and couldn't drive me as often. My parents, realizing that I was a full-blown skate nut, did what came naturally for them—they made sure I made it to the park as often as possible.

A few times a week my dad would drive me to Oasis after school and watch me skate for hours, until the park closed, and then we'd drive back home. My mom was always available if my dad was busy. Many times they'd drop whatever they were doing to drive me to the skatepark.

Skating at Oasis forced me to get my first job—a paper route—so I could make money to help pay for my park pass and new skateboards. It turned out to be the only "real" job I've ever had besides skateboarding.

My dad (apparently happier than me) at one of my contest winnings.

5: NO MORE TEARS

My mom tells me she is grateful to skateboarding because instead of giving them a hard time, I directed my energy at improving my skating. I was still hyper, but there would be no more crazed games of tennis. My brother said I mellowed out when I played arcade games with him.

I did other sports besides skating. I played basketball and baseball. My dad was the president of the baseball league and coach of our basketball team, and he did what he could to make sure the leagues were the best they could be. That's what made my decision to stop playing team sports so hard.

One day my dad picked me up from Oasis and drove me straight to basketball practice. I was in such a hurry that I forgot to take my kneepads off. I was running around the court in skateboarding safety equipment. My dad called me over, and I took off my pads. I looked at him, and was scared because of what I had to say.

"Dad, I'd rather skate than play basketball or baseball. I have more fun skating, and I feel like getting better."

I expected him to freak out, after all the energy he'd put into the leagues. But he already knew what I was telling him.

"Fine by me," he answered. With that reply, my jock days were officially over.

WISING UP

Now that school was my only distraction, all I ever did was skateboard. I didn't see any of my old, nonskater friends, because I spent every spare minute at Oasis. Life at the skatepark was a different world. Even though I was younger than most of the local skaters, everybody treated me as an equal—as a skater. Some of the best skateboarders in the world practiced there, and I would watch them and try to learn from them. I'd imitate them and occasionally ask them for help.

A weird side effect happened once I started skating nonstop— I became nicer. I remember thinking one day, "I'm tired of being a jerk to my parents." Skating made me focus on improving myself rather than dwelling on my immature frustrations. With skating my teammates couldn't blame me for losing—because I didn't have any. I only had myself to blame. The unfortunate part of this was that I became constantly annoyed with myself for not living up to my expectations. That was the worst feeling ever.

I'd practice a single trick for hours straight. I'd fall, analyze what I did wrong, and then try it again. I did this like a broken record until I landed a trick. If I messed up, I'd solve the problem by watching other skaters or concentrating harder on the trick. I'd even think about improving as I went to sleep.

The only "person" I ever turned to with my problems was my new best friend, Zorro. One day after school, I found him digging around in a trash can. I stopped to play with him and took him home. My parents said I could keep the black-and-white cat, who at the time didn't have a name.

My dad named him Zorro because of his facial markings, and he quickly showed that he had as much attitude as I used to. He was never afraid to pop his claws out and start slashing if someone tried to pick him up. I was the only one in the house who could pet him. (Not knowing this, one visiting skater tried to pet Zorro and was soon running around the house screaming with Zorro attached to his arm and slashing away.) He was my faithful companion for the next decade until he died in the early '90s.

Zorro, my favorite cat and companion, and me mugging for the camera.

6: THE BASICS

I practiced at Oasis and learned all the basic skateboard tricks such as rock 'n' rolls and grinds. But once I tried to learn more advanced moves, like airs, I ran into a problem. I was too skinny. I had to wear elbow pads on my knees, because I was so skinny that nothing else would fit. I wore the smallest pads possible on my elbows, which were still too large and were constantly slipping down.

I was too light to grab airs early like everybody else. I had to work extra hard to get enough speed to propel myself out of the bowl, and if I bent down to grab, I would lose my momentum. The only way I could figure out how to do airs was to pop an ollie and, once I was in the air, grab my board. At the time, it looked weird. Nobody else did anything like it. I was embarrassed about not being able to skate like everybody else—other skaters made fun of me and called me a "circus skater." Little did I know that in ten years, they and every other skater would be doing airs using my technique.

When I decided to learn a trick, nothing could get in my way. Like the time I was learning Inverts. I knew I was close to landing one, but my dad had come to pick me up for dinner. I asked him to give me a few more tries. Then a few more. It became obvious to my dad that I wasn't going to leave before I landed one. Half an hour later he had to pick me up kicking and screaming and drag me to the car. I glared at him. "Dad! If you'd just let me try it five hundred more times I would have had it!"

FIRST CONTEST

I was eleven years old when I entered my first contest. It was at Oasis, but I was still scared. I almost made myself sick from nerves. I was so freaked out that I couldn't speak. During the drive to the skatepark I went over and over in my mind all the ways I could goof up. The closer we drove to the skatepark, the more I thought about telling my parents I was too sick to skate. My skateboard career almost ended before it started!

It seemed as if there were thousands of skaters entered in the contest. They came from all over Southern California to skate. I had never seen so many people at Oasis. The park was so full that it was impossible to practice. When they finally called my name to skate, I was so nervous I fell on the easy tricks. I never found out how I did, because the contest took so long that we left before the results were posted.

TREASURE MAPS

I discovered *SkateBoarder* magazine at this time. I was blown away that there was a magazine dedicated to skating, but the thing that really impressed me were the pictures of kids my age ripping! On top of that, *SkateBoarder* had skatepark coupons. I realized that there were ten different skateparks within a two-hour drive. I had thought Oasis was the only skatepark around! My dad began driving me to different ones every weekend. It helped me improve, because I got used to riding in different terrains.

At one skatepark I saw two professional skaters whom I looked up to, Duane Peters and Steve Alba. Unlike the pros at Oasis, or my hero Eddie Elguera, these two were known for being "punk." They were joking around and laughing. I wanted them to think I was cool, so I laughed with them. Suddenly they stopped and Duane walked over to me. They weren't laughing anymore. Duane spat on the ground by my feet and said, "This is punk rock, kid." Steve laughed in the background. I was crushed. I didn't even want to skate the rest of the day.

Once I discovered all the different skateparks, I began competing in the Association of Skatepark Owners (ASPO) contest series, which took place a few weekends a month. I began figuring out little tricks to help me skate well and control my nervousness. I'd draw a diagram of the skatepark I was going to skate and imagine the tricks I would do during the contest. I marked an X on the spot where I would do the trick and wrote a list of tricks on the side of the paper. This way even when I wasn't skating, I could work on my contest run by visualizing it until I had it memorized.

I was a perfectionist. Even if I won a contest, I'd get mad at myself if I missed a trick or sketched on one that I had wired. Other times I skated as well as I knew I could, and even though I didn't win, I was still happy with myself. My mom says she could never tell how I placed at a contest by my attitude. If I was upset with myself, I wouldn't make eye contact or speak with anybody. I'd grab Zorro, take him upstairs, and lie on my bed petting him and thinking about how I'd messed up.

By the end of the year I had won my age division. But what was most important to me, I was being invited to skate on the Oasis Skatepark team. Now I could skate for free! Every weekday after school my dad would drive me to Oasis, and I'd skate until 8:00 at night.

"Hi, Dad, no need to rush if you're coming to pick me up."

Learning inverts back in 1983.
It was hard to stay up there with wristguards on.

An early lien air in 1983 while the pro skater Billy Ruff watched.

7: OUT OF STYLE

Soon after I joined the Oasis team, skating started to lose its popularity. Skate friends suddenly stopped coming to Oasis and I never saw them again. Skateparks began to close down, so my weekend trips to other parks stopped. I skated only at Oasis. Even Oasis, which had been jammed full of skaters only a few months earlier, looked like a ghost town.

I was an eleven-year-old skateboard freak, and there was only one other skater at school. We would arrive half an hour early and skate a curb before classes. We didn't look like the other students. I looked like a mummy who couldn't afford all his wrappings. I was covered in scabs and always had Band-Aids stuck on me or Ace bandages wrapped around a sore wrist or knee.

DAD TO THE RESCUE

The one positive aspect of skateboarding losing popularity was that the community became closer. If there was a contest at Oasis, my dad would invite out-of-town skaters to stay at our house. One time he invited the team manager of Dogtown Skateboards to stay over. She saw me skate and passed the word on, and Dogtown gave me a free skateboard. A few months later the Dogtown crew saw me skate again and thought I had improved enough to be invited to join their team.

By this time skateboarding was so unpopular that the ASPO went out of business. My dad saw that amateur skaters, the few that were left, wouldn't have a structured contest series anymore. Just like he had with my brothers and sisters, Dad decided to jump in and help out. He figured since he'd organized my brother Steve's Little League, he could do the same for me. With four other people he started the California Amateur Skateboard League, better known as CASL, which still runs contests today. He even dragged my mom in and made her a scorekeeper and timer. It was a family affair that, even though I appreciated it, would create a lot of conflict between us as I grew older.

VIOLIN VERSUS SKATEBOARDING

The only thing I really loved outside of skateboarding was playing the violin. I had started playing it in band and loved the fact that it was so complicated, for me at least. It reminded me a lot of skating, because it was something I could do on my own. I must have been a weird-looking sight—imagine a bony kid, wrapped in Ace bandages and covered with scabs, playing the violin. I didn't care. I loved it.

But in a fight over my spare time, the violin got its butt whipped. I was skating so much that all my free time was devoted to it. Even though I enjoyed playing the violin, I knew I had to make a choice. My violin teacher was angry when I told him I was quitting for skating. He tried to get my mom to make me change my mind. She knew better than that and always supported whatever I wanted to do, as long as it wasn't harmful. She loved skating and all my colorful skate friends who would stay at the house, and they seemed to enjoy time with my parents, who knew more about skateboarding than a lot of skaters.

Now that I'm thirty-three years old, I've decided to give the violin a second chance. A friend recently gave me a violin, and I'm planning on taking lessons again.

My dad and me at Virginia Beach, 1986. He was very supportive of my skating, but as a teenager, sometimes I wished he wasn't as involved.

OASIS DRIES UP

My parents had decided to move about forty minutes away from Oasis, but luckily one of the few remaining skateparks was only a few miles away. It was called Del Mar Skate Ranch. I had skated there a few times before, but I hated the place. The pool felt weird, because I was used to Oasis. But favorite parks or not, I liked skating with people, and Del Mar always had a few locals to skate with. I stopped going to Oasis and skated Del Mar every day.

Skateparks back then were a lot different than they are today. There were no "sessions" where you pay to skate for a few hours and then leave. I would buy a pass and skate all day long on the weekends or after school. I hung out there even if I wasn't skating. Del Mar became a clubhouse for all the skaters who felt uncomfortable in the outside world. We could goof around playing skate tag or video games, or read skate magazines and argue about who was the best skater in the world. (I knew it was Steve Caballero.) There was a trailer park next to the skatepark, and we'd sneak in and use its pool. I figured out what school bus from my high school dropped kids off closest to Del Mar. I pretended I was being dropped off at my home, and then I would skate a mile to the park. I made new friends, who I'm still friends with today, and it became one of the most enjoyable times of my life.

MOST IMPROVED SKATER

By the end of the year I had skated well enough in most CASL contests to win the Most Improved Skater Award. I drove with my dad to the CASL awards banquet early, because he had to set up the tables and PA system. While he did that, I skated to the store with a friend to get a soda. I was so excited about the awards ceremony that I didn't notice the massive crack in the sidewalk. My board jerked to a stop, but I continued to go forward. The next thing I remembered was waking up on an unknown lady's porch with a headache. She lived in front of the monster crack and took care of me while my friend skated back to get my dad.

My dad had to run the CASL awards ceremony and couldn't drive me home, so I waited in the car as he hurried through as fast as he could. Every once in a while, I would open the car door to throw up from my concussion. An hour later he ran out, handed me my trophy, congratulated me, and drove me home.

Backside ollie in 1980 at Del Mar. At first I hated Del Mar, but I grew to love it.

8: THE BONES BRIGADE

Stacy Peralta was the world champion skateboarder in 1977. He was famous all over the world and had one of the smoothest and most innovative styles around. After breaking both his wrists, he retired and started a skateboard company with George Powell, which was called Powell and Peralta. He recruited the best skaters to be on the Powell and Peralta team, and called it the Bones Brigade. It was one of the best teams in the history of skating. In the early '80s, this was *the* team to be on. On it was one of my favorite skaters, Steve Caballero, the most inventive skater around.

I remember the first time Stacy came up and said hi to me at a contest. I couldn't believe it! Stacy knew who I was! He asked how Dogtown was treating me.

"Fine, I guess," I stammered back. I didn't even really know how a sponsored skateboarder was supposed to be treated. They sporadically sent me free stuff, but that was it.

"Good. I like your skating." He smiled and left.

I was so happy about being noticed and complimented from a legend like Stacy that I can't remember the rest of the contest at all.

One night, at the end of the year, Stacy called me up at home.

"You know, Tony, Dogtown went out of business." It was the first I had heard of it. Suddenly I was going to be back to square one and buying boards, I thought.

"If you could come up here to Marina, we could talk about sponsorship," he said.

I went up and skated for him. Suddenly I was sponsored again. Stacy told me later that he'd already made up his mind after seeing me skating in a contest in Marina near his house. I had a good run, and I may even have won the contest (I can't remember). I walked away from the contest angry with myself. He said I had a look of disgust on my face, like I was furious with myself, and he couldn't understand why. He eventually figured out that I was rarely happy with my skating. He said it was my "fierce determination" that made him put me on the Bones Brigade.

But I had a problem. Another company had already asked me to skate for them and given me a huge box of free skate equipment. My dad sat me down and explained that it wasn't right for me to take free skate equipment from one company while I was thinking about riding for another. I called up a guy from the first company and thanked him for offering me a place on their team, but told him

I had decided to skate for Stacy. It was a decision that would affect my entire life in ways I couldn't understand at the time.

Next to my parents, Stacy was my biggest supporter. He was one of the most positive influences on my life. He encouraged and helped direct my skating in ways I'd never thought possible.

ROOKIE HAZING

When I met Steve Caballero, I was awestruck. I had always looked up to him, and now we were on the same team. My first year on the Bones Brigade, I was nervous around him, because I thought he was so awesome. It was like meeting a superstar actor. The first time we spent time together was at Stacy's apartment in Los Angeles. Mike McGill, another Bones Brigade skater whom I admired, and Steve were in the apartment complex's hot tub. I wanted to make an impression on them, and make them like me in some way. Steve was chewing gum and accidentally dropped it in the hot tub.

"What would you do if I ate that?" I blurted out, ready to do anything to make them remember me.

"What? If you just chewed the gum? I don't know, maybe I'd clap," Steve answered.

I knew I had to do something quick to let them know how special I was.

"No, I don't mean 'just out of the water.' I mean—"

"Out from between my toes," Steve said with a laugh.

"Yeah!" I exclaimed.

Steve wrapped the long string of gum around his toes like a spider's web and waved his foot at me. I carefully picked the gum out as Steve and Mike winced. I chewed it and blew a bubble as they clapped. I couldn't have been happier—they liked me!

SLOW START

Once I was on the Powell team, they started sending me to contests. While I had been doing well in local contests and winning my age division, now I was in a completely different league—the sponsored amateurs. This is one step below being a professional.

Stacy flew me and the rest of the Bones Brigade to a contest in Florida. I was thirteen years old, the youngest member of the Bones Brigade. I was so intimidated that I barely spoke to anybody. To make matters worse, there was a massive storm blowing once we got off the plane. I was used to wimpy California weather, but storms on the East Coast are very different. Fat lightning bolts zorched down, making the sky bright as day for a few seconds. Thunder boomed so loud that I thought I could feel myself shaking. The rain fell so hard, it was like standing in a shower. I was so scared I couldn't sleep that night. I thought lightning was going to fry our hotel room.

The weather cleared up for the contest, but I wished it hadn't. It was my first time competing as a Bones Brigade member and all I wanted was to impress everybody, but I failed. I skated horribly. I thought I let everyone down. I felt so crappy that I could barely look Stacy in the eyes. He knew I would skate poorly but wanted me to get a taste of how much I had to push myself to diversify my skills. It worked. I wanted to get as good as every skater at that contest, and I would try that much harder.

My friend and closest competitor during the '80s, Christian Hosoi.

Steve Caballero was one of my early inspirations and later became my teammate. Here, we're hanging out during a contest in the mid-'80s.

Making funny faces at the camera while doing an invert—not a good idea.

9: FACEPLANTS

As I improved my skating skills, I also improved my ability to slam—and I got pretty good at it. But bashing my face into concrete was the least of my problems. I would gladly have done that every day if it meant I didn't have to go to school. It wasn't the schoolwork or the teachers who stressed me out so much; it was my schoolmates.

I got picked on. I was less than five feet tall when I entered eighth grade, and weighed less than eighty pounds. I was so skinny that I resembled a set of toothpicks walking awkwardly down the hallway. Only my legs had a hint of muscle on them. If I flexed my bicep nothing would pop up—muscle or fat. And, I was short. If I had to be skinny, at least someone could have given me height. I was a seriously late bloomer and in school nothing is more noticeable than that. Leaving the comforts of elementary school and going to a huge high school kept me up at night worrying. At my

Filming on the ramp for *The Search for Animal Chin* in 1986. Quadruple inverts by Mike McGill, Steve Caballero, Lance Mountain, and me.

old school, my teacher had let me teach the class about skate-boarding by bringing in film that my dad had shot of me. I could tell nobody in my new school was going to be that encouraging. Serra High was a notoriously rough high school that admitted eighth and ninth graders. I was entering the lowest grade in a massive school, and I was more scared than I'd ever been. I looked as if I'd mistaken a high school for my elementary school.

To make matters worse, I was a skateboard nut. I was the sole skater in Serra High. Nobody could figure out why I looked so ratty, with torn-up clothes and shoes. The fact that I was sponsored by the skateboard team of my dreams meant nothing to my classmates. I was considered a loser geek who still participated in a silly fad that everybody knew was "out." I had no friends at school. But after a while it didn't bother me too much. Sometimes the jocks on the football team would pick me up and spin me around if they saw me in the hallways, but I soon mastered the art of blending into the walls. I would arrive just as the last bell was ringing and be the first one out the door.

I got in trouble once because of my competitiveness. We were playing a game of flag football in gym class. As I understood the rules, that meant there was no physical contact. Instead of tackling a player, you are supposed to tear the flag off of them. I had the ball by some fluke, and I knew I could run fast enough to score a touchdown. I whipped around the largest kid in class, a hulking ogre who always bugged me. He gave chase, but I was too quick. I sprinted down the field and scored a touchdown. I turned around, happy finally to be involved in some sort of winning school activity. That's when I saw this monster running full charge at me. He hit me square in the stomach, knocking me off my feet like I was a bug on his windshield. I landed on my back, gasping for air. The bully got up, swept the grass off his knees, and walked away. But even as I was wheezing I managed a little smile to myself—at least I had beat him and scored the touchdown.

10: CHECK THE BOX

I skated in a few more amateur contests and, with Stacy's coaching, improved. Stacy told me he knew I had the talent; I just needed to learn how to skate contests better. He helped me plan my routines so that I started and ended with my best tricks and made a lasting impact on the judges.

Contests then weren't the big deal they are now. In the early 1980s there were so few skaters and even fewer fans that contest crowds were made up mostly of relatives and friends. There were less than fifty professional skaters in the world, whereas now there are hundreds. A skater can win over $20,000 in a contest today, but back then you only made a hundred dollars, and that was if you placed in the top three. If you placed fourth, you didn't win anything.

In 1982, a few months after my fourteenth birthday, I turned pro. Most of my friends with whom I skated in amateur contests had already turned pro, and Stacy felt that I was ready. It was at a contest in Whittier, California, that Stacy asked me casually if I'd like to turn pro.

I looked at him and said, "I don't know. Should I?"

"I don't want to tell you either way," he replied. "It's definitely up to you."

I knew Stacy wouldn't have asked me if he didn't think I was ready. I hadn't seriously considered turning pro until then. The goals I constantly set for myself in skating were always about improving, I didn't have any other objectives. Being a pro skater wasn't a career at that time. A skater could barely make enough to survive, because skating was dead. I was young, living at home, and got all the skateboarding equipment I wanted for free. What did I need cash for?

As I filled out my contest registration, I stared at the two boxes near the bottom of the sheet. One said "amateur" and the other said "professional." I put an X in the pro box and that was that. I placed third in the contest, and when I told my parents that their youngest son was now a professional, they smiled and said, "That's nice."

SAN DIEGUITO JAIL

Nobody inside or outside skating seemed to take notice of my professional debut. I was miserable at school, and even though I never complained to my parents, they knew I was going through torture at Serra High. Luckily, we moved to Cardiff. I couldn't have been happier—a new school.

I was in for a rude awakening. San Dieguito High included grades nine to twelve. Once again, I was at the bottom of the classes. Never mind that I still looked at least three years younger than everybody else. As depressing as Serra had been for me, San Dieguito was worse. It was known as one of the roughest schools in the area. Bullying jocks and wannabe gang members picked on me from the start. Sometimes I would walk down the hallways and they'd pick me up, spin me around, and put me back down again while other students laughed. The only thing good about San Dieguito was that Miki Vuckovich, the only other skater at the school, went there. Finally, at long last, I had a friend at school. We suffered and skated together.

Believe it or not, I had a huge appetite as a kid—still do. A stickman acid drop two decades ago. Nice shorts!

Fakie ollie on my first pro board. Del Mar, 1983.

11: CHEATING

I had other problems besides school. Because I ollied into my tricks, other skaters made fun of me. At Del Mar, when I was skating with my friends, we all had fun and nobody cared, but at a contest it was a different story. A lot of my fellow professionals laughed at me and my new style. There was nothing I could do about it. One skater whom I admired called me a cheater because I ollied into my airs and it made different grabs easier. Stacy told me not to worry what anybody thought. He said I was developing my own style of skating. Even back then he believed I had the potential to create tricks that nobody else could do.

Skating was changing and the emphasis was on tricks. Luckily, I had a lot of those. What I didn't have was the aggressive style that most other skaters possessed. People started calling me a "robot," and they didn't mean it as a compliment. But, on the other hand, a lot of older skaters couldn't learn enough of the new tricks to keep up with the changing style.

Robot or not, judges at contests appreciated the amount of tricks I could jam into a run, and I won the next pro contest. It took place at Del Mar, which I knew like the back of my hand. Ironically, one of the people I beat was the same pro who had spat at my feet years before. But winning the contest didn't boost my popularity at school. A local news station did a small story on me, and a classmate who saw it and knew that I skated asked me if I "knew that Tony Hawk who skated at Del Mar."

I told him that I was "that Tony Hawk."

He shook his head and said, "Yeah? Really? Well, you sure don't look like that dude."

I became even more depressed than I had been at Serra. I thought about leaving San Dieguito, so in tenth grade I took and passed the high school equivalency exam, which would have allowed me to graduate early. At that point I would have done anything to escape the hassles of that school. But I knew my parents would be disappointed. They wanted to see me graduate traditionally, ceremony and all. My only other option was to switch schools, so my parents and I asked the principal at Torrey Pines if I could cross districts and attend his school. He had heard of me and respected what I had accomplished in skating. He knew I had good grades, so he invited me to go there. As I walked out of his office, I felt as if the weight of the world had been lifted from my shoulders. Imagine—a school where the principal was hip enough to know about skating.

SKATEBOARDING

Doing a lien air in 1984. Believe it or not, this used to be considered a large crowd at a contest—and skating was popular at the time!

Gymnast plant at Del Mar Skate Ranch, my home away from home.

12: THE PARENT TRAP

I will be the first to admit that I wouldn't have been this successful without the enthusiastic support of my parents, but I'd be lying if I claimed that it didn't cause problems when I was growing up. After my dad had helped get CASL up and running, he turned his attention to the professional skateboard contest circuit. At the time, pro contests weren't unified and there was no ranking system. So, in 1983, he started the National Skateboarding Association (NSA) to fix some of the problems.

Skaters and people involved in the industry appreciated what my dad was doing, but I felt the pressure right away. I was a relatively new pro, and my dad was running the official contest series. Once again my mom became the official time- and scorekeeper to keep costs down (she worked for free). People started whispering that contests might be fixed in my favor.

My dad's gruff way of dealing with people didn't always help.

Picture Oscar the Grouch from *Sesame Street,* take away the green fur and give him a larger nose, and you have my dad. He'd yell at skaters for practicing when they weren't supposed to or for goofing off. I had always been basically well behaved at contests and he rarely had any excuse to yell at me, so sometimes it seemed as if he was favoring me. Eventually, skaters realized that he cared about them, and he just communicated by pretending he was a tough guy who grumbled and complained all the time. His bark was a lot worse than his bite.

THE WORST-SELLING BOARD EVER?

Stacy told me to think about ideas for my first professional board. I had a friend draw up a picture of a hawk swooping down and gave it to Stacy. Unfortunately, I didn't let Stacy know that it was just an idea, so it was printed on my boards, almost exactly as it was drawn. It wasn't the coolest graphic—everyone else had things like skulls and crosses; I had something from the Discovery Channel. In 1983 I sold one board in my first month as a pro. One person in the entire world liked me enough to buy my deck. I made a whopping 85 cents. A few months later I had upped my sales to five decks and almost made five bucks. But I didn't care. What did I need money for? My house and board were covered.

NEW AND IMPROVED

Stacy decided to kill the swooping hawk and create a new graphic for me. A Powell artist showed me what they had come up with—a hawk skull in front of an iron cross. Don't ask me what it meant, but I loved it. My friends and I would jokingly call it the "screaming chicken skull." The royalty checks for my board instantly improved. Now I was getting a consistent $500 to $1,000 a month. That was serious cash for a fifteen-year-old. It was like winning the lottery.

Stacy was making other changes, too. He decided to create a skateboard video. There had been videos before, but never one focusing on a team and showcasing modern skating. The entire Bones Brigade crew filmed for a month, and we all watched it for the first time after a Del Mar contest while sitting on my sofa, eating chips, and drinking soda.

I put my board to good use that summer and traveled around the United States doing demos with other Bones Brigaders. I won a contest in Florida. I was proud of that because I had skated so poorly the last time I had been there. My win meant that I was learning how to skate different ramps and bowls. But mostly I bounced all over the results. Sometimes I won and skated the best I could, and sometimes I couldn't stay on my board if I was Krazy Glued to it. I needed to learn to skate consistently, no matter what park it was.

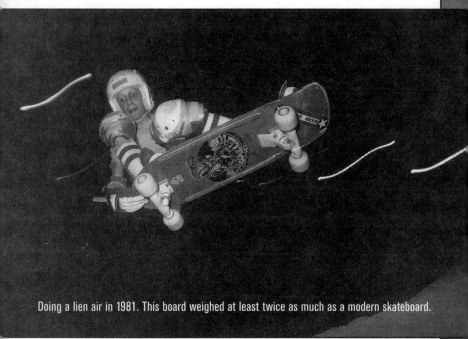

Doing a lien air in 1981. This board weighed at least twice as much as a modern skateboard.

Fakie ollie with my first board graphic, which was not a good seller.

Don't look up my shorts. A Japan air at Del Mar, 1985.

13: COOL SCHOOL

I couldn't have been happier once I skated onto the Torrey Pines school property. It was close to the beach and surfers hung out in the parking lot. Nobody vibed me at all. No one even seemed to notice my strange clothes and bleached blond hair. Most of the surfers also had a similar look.

Things got even better—this school had *two* skaters. We didn't get hassled. That year I turned sixteen and bought my mom's old Honda Civic. As a birthday present, my parents had it painted red. Now I could drive to school and the skatepark. I didn't really date much because I was too busy skating. I spent every spare minute at Del Mar or goofing around with my skate buddies.

Torrey Pines was great, but I was still the invisible boy at school. I was enrolled in advanced math and English, and maintained a solid grade point average. But most important, that was the year my friends and I discovered independent studies. According to school rules, we could make up a physical education program to take as long as the teacher felt it was something we could learn from. The three of us wrote an outline describing "Skateboard PE." We explained how we had to train by doing railslides and popping ollies. It was ridiculous—you don't "train" when you skate—but it got our point across. The teachers okayed the idea, so we spent our regular gym class at the skatepark and we got credit on our report card for it. All we needed to do was have Grant Brittain, the manager at Del Mar, sign a paper saying we skated during our "class time."

MCFRUSTRATION

Everything in my world that year changed during a contest at Del Mar. Mike McGill blew everybody out of the water when he unveiled the McTwist during his run. It was a 540-degree spin with a flip in it. Nothing like that had ever been done in skateboarding. It became the trick that defined the new era of vert skating. It was a dividing point between skaters. In a few months there were skaters who could land a McTwist and those who couldn't. Eventually, you had to do one in your run to win a contest.

After that contest almost every vert skater went home and practiced the McTwist. I spent every afternoon and all day on the weekends at Del Mar trying to land it. I started to go a little insane, because I became so frustrated with myself. After a month of failed attempts, it was all I could think about. In school I'd doodle absent-mindedly and look down at my work to see that I'd written "Pull a McTwist." I'd picture myself doing it, trying to figure out the key that would allow me to land it. I slammed so many times that I became scared of even trying it, which only made me madder. I forced myself to keep going.

After two months, I finally landed one. It was the most awkward sight you can imagine. My butt was so low it scraped the bottom of the pool, my feet were hanging off the board, and I wobbled all over trying to keep my balance. But I had landed one, and once I knew I could do it, the trick became a lot easier.

WORLD CHAMPION

Contests were becoming more fun for me. I learned something before every one. I'd always brainstorm ways to create a better, more exciting run. Even though I enjoyed winning, I was still frustrated with myself a lot of the time when I didn't skate as well as I knew I could have. They were also fun because I was friends with most of the pros, and going to a contest meant that we could all hang out for a weekend and everything was paid for by our sponsors. Contests were like the perfect vacation, and I got to have at least ten of them a year.

There was one contest in 1984 that wasn't too much fun. It was called "The Booney Ramp Bang," and it took place on a ramp in the desert. A fellow pro, Neil Blender, did an invert on the deck right in front of me. I thought he might crash into me, so I backed up. Unfortunately, whoever built the ramp had decided that guardrails were not a needed safety precaution. I found myself waving my arms and doing a perfect imitation of Wile E. Coyote after he runs off a cliff. Neil, seeing that I'd backed off the ramp, tried to catch me, but all he did was grab a leg, which flipped me into the air. I did a quarter-flip and landed ten feet below on my back. I got the air knocked out of me. I guess I was a little lucky, since I just missed hitting a glass Gatorade bottle that was on the ground a few inches to my right. Had I landed there, I'd have been picking glass out of my back.

I didn't even come close to winning every contest that year, but I won a few and placed high enough in the others to have more points than anybody else. I was awarded the NSA's first world vert champion title.

A lot of people still made fun of my style. I hated it and would have changed it if I could have. To hear fellow pro skaters ripping on it behind my back made me even more bummed. My friends

Chris Miller and Christian Hosoi didn't do as many tricks as I did, but they had the best styles in skateboarding. They looked super smooth when they skated, almost as if they were surfing the ramp instead of skating it. Everybody loved watching them skate. I tried to change my style, but the way you skate is the hardest thing to change. It can evolve as you grow, but to ask your body to relearn how to look when you're skating is impossible. Because I couldn't change that, I concentrated on the things I could change, such as inventing new tricks.

Steve Caballero, popping a fakie ollie while I admire his technique. Pomona, 1983.

14: BALANCING ACT

I spent the summer between my sophomore and junior years skating in contests and touring around the world with the Bones Brigade. Skating's popularity was increasing quickly. I was making more money than my parents and teachers. My dad ran the NSA on a slim budget and barely paid himself at all.

When I returned to school, my schedule didn't slow down. Winning the world championships made me one of the most popular skaters, and every other weekend I was taking a day off from school to attend demos or contests. Most of my teachers understood my situation, but for the first time my grades started to slip.

I had to drop out of advanced classes because the workload was too heavy. But I still kept my grade point average up as high as I could so that I could get into a decent college. Nobody made a career out of skating. I knew I would have to get a "real" job someday; it was only a matter of time.

After years of skating contests I finally had enough confidence and tricks to start winning consistently. I won my second NSA world champion title, and after winning contests at Del Mar, Upland, and Virginia Beach, I became the first pro to win three contests in a row.

Even though skating was becoming more popular, nonskaters were clueless about it. There were no skating movies, no video games, or X Games. At school, only the two other skaters were aware that I was pro. It was weird—I'd skate a demo for thousands of fans and sign autographs for hours afterwards, and then return back to school an unknown.

My mouth was stuck like this for a day (a mild version of lockjaw) after a serious bout with food poisoning. I still managed to skate. Brazil, 1987.

15: DAD SLAMS

Over the years people have commented that I'm reserved, but they have to understand that I learned from the grand master. One night when I was sixteen years old, I thought I was spending a regular night at home watching TV with my dad, since my mom was at school (she eventually earned her doctorate when she was in her sixties).

Suddenly, he grabbed his chest. "Um, Tony?" he asked as my eyes were glued to the TV screen. I looked over at him and saw him gritting his teeth.

"Yeah?" I answered.

"I think I'm having a heart attack. Maybe you'd better call an ambulance."

I freaked and started jumping around. My dad was waving me down, telling me to calm down and call the ambulance. I called 911 and we waited the longest five minutes of my life.

This was it, I thought, my dad's life was leaving him like water going down a drain. I had precious little time left with him, and I had to let him know that I was sorry for all the bratty things I'd ever done to him. I had to let him know how much I appreciated his support. We had had a few massive fights about him being too involved in my life. Sometimes I had just wanted to skate with my friends at a contest and not have him around. I felt that sometimes he pushed himself into my life. But I knew how much he helped skateboarding, so it was a trade-off. Most important, I had to let him know I loved him.

This was my moment—I had to let him know what he meant to me before he died! I opened up like I never have before, and expressed my love.

"Dad," I said. "I want you to know I love you."

"Yeah, I know," he said matter-of-factly. I waited for his declaration of love. I was ready.

"Dad, I said I loved you," I repeated.

"I heard you. I know you do."

"I want to thank you for all you've done for me."

"Okay. You're welcome."

"Dad—"

"Hey, is that the ambulance I hear?"

The ambulance finally did come and took Dad to the hospital. He recovered quickly and went back to being his loving, gruff self and running the NSA. For a man in his sixties who was over-worked, had an extra twenty pounds around his gut, was diabetic, listed Sizzler as his favorite restaurant, and ordered prime rib by the pound, he was asking for health problems. But nothing as fee-ble as a heart attack was going to take him out.

After a short stay in the hospital, Dad was released and had to take a handful of pills daily. But the pills never slowed down his Sizzler intake, and he refused to stop working.

CRAZY CAMP

I finished my junior year with Bs across my report card. I was invited to skate and teach at a summer camp in Sweden over the vacation with fellow Bones Brigader Lance Mountain, and I accepted eagerly. I thought a few weeks in a warm camp with a nice ramp would be perfect. I couldn't have been more wrong. Lance and I slowly went insane from being stuck in one place for too long. We had no transportation and no city to distract us, because the camp was in the boonies. We had to solve the problem. I bummed a ride into the city and bought a car for $500 from a used car dealership.

The car was awesome. Lance, the more talented artist, painted it with various Powell logos. We drove it like stuntmen through a nearby field. Once we even took it on the beach and spun donuts all afternoon. Sometimes we'd get carried away and take it to the nearby forest for some off-roading. (This car was definitely not designed for the dirt.) Lance drove like a professional, swerving around trees and bouncing over dirt mounds. Eventually the car died and we pushed it back to the dealership and left it there at night. My friend from Sweden said that he saw the car, fixed up and painted a different color, for sale a few weeks later.

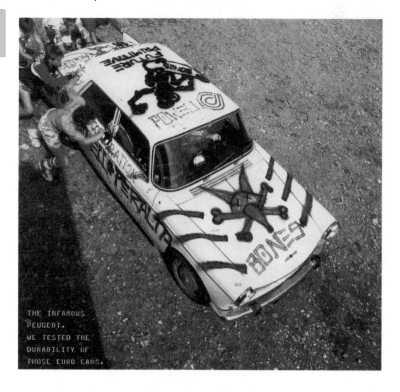

THE INFAMOUS PEUGEOT. WE TESTED THE DURABILITY OF THOSE EURO CARS.

16: FUTURE PRIMITIVE

The success of the first Bones Brigade video encouraged Stacy to make another one, which he called *Future Primitive.* We filmed for a few months and had a real movie theater premiere in Los Angeles. At the time, it blew away every other skate video with its originality and quality. It captured the fun of skating perfectly. But the most important part occurred when we weren't filming. Stacy had driven down to Del Mar, and while we were taking a lunch break, we talked about the tricks we'd filmed so far. Stacy, between bites of his sandwich, said, "You have the talent to win any contest you want from now on."

I was blown away. Stacy wasn't one to say things just to make you happy; he meant what he said. I was knocked speechless, because it meant so much coming from him. It gave me even more motivation to keep improving.

FREEDOM

My last year of school was rough. My grades dropped because I was so busy with skating. I was forced to balance my homework with my crazy schedule. It went from demos every other weekend to being in a contest and at least two demos a month. I would fly all over the world on the weekends and be back in school on a Monday or a Tuesday, so I missed a lot of classes.

At the end of the year I won another NSA world championship title, but still nobody at school had a clue about what I did. That is, until I did a small Mountain Dew commercial. It aired on TV the last month of school and everybody saw it. Suddenly I was famous. People I'd never talked to before started conversations with me in the hallway. It was weird after being ignored all those years. I wasn't bitter; I just wasn't used to it.

I became even more popular when I got my own place. I was told that for tax purposes, I should invest my skateboard money in a home. I found a house a few miles away from my parents and bought it a few months before graduation. My mom was bummed. She tried to convince me not to move out, because she loved hanging out with all my skate friends. She said she'd miss all the different hair colors and hairstyles my friends had.

After graduation, I went on a U.S. tour with the Bones Brigade. Now I could fully enjoy the life of a professional skateboarder. Until then I had been the only skater on the team still in high school and had missed a lot of events because of it.

I'm trying a tweaked backside boneless at Del Mar. I thought that pulling my socks all the way up would help my kneepads stay on—it didn't always work.

Tweaking a layback air in 1983. Stacy Peralta once called me "noodly." I wonder why?

17: WINNING CONTESTS IS NOT ALWAYS FUN

The year after *Future Primitive* came out, Stacy started filming his most ambitious video, *The Search for Animal Chin*. This would be more like a movie starring the Bones Brigade packed with tons of skating. We filmed in Hawaii, Las Vegas, and all over California. The point of this video was to show skaters, who had gotten wrapped up in getting sponsored or being better than their friends, that skating was about having fun. A lot of people tell me that *Chin* is their favorite skate video of all time.

I needed to listen to what Stacy was saying in his video, because skating contests were quickly losing their appeal for me. By the end of the year I had won my fourth NSA world championship title and seemed to win a majority of the contests. But after a few years of pushing myself to create the best contest runs I could, I burned out. It had gotten to the point where I was expected to win. If I skated into second place, even if I had a good run, people said I "lost."

It really hit home when one skater told me during a contest that he didn't even think about winning, he was happy getting second place to me. I had won every vert world championship title since the start of the NSA. But it was too much pressure for me. I felt that some skaters, and most of the judges, had unfair expectations of me and my skating. Even though I often won, I had to outperform myself, not other competitors. Each contest run had to be better than the last for me to score the same. One of the head judges told me later how he had to instruct the other judges to score me fairly. He said other judges thought that a 720 from me should be scored the same as a 540 from somebody else.

I was miserable and started to get depressed. I spoke to Stacy about quitting contests. To my surprise, he supported me. He understood the pressures that went along with being world champion, because he had once been one. Even though I was Powell's most popular skater at the time, due in large part to my contest results, he wanted me to be happy. Both of us were unsure of what lay ahead if I stopped competing. Would I continue to be able to make a living? Would I have to get another job? Would Powell lose money?

He told me that if I ever decided to compete again, I should keep my practice mellow so that nobody would know what to expect in my run. It would be fresh for them. He later told me that he knew I'd return to competition.

MY OWN WONDERLAND

I won another NSA vert world championship title and decided to stop skating contests. I made some other big changes in my life. I bought a house in Fallbrook, a desert town far away from the beach cities where I had always lived. I would miss the beach, but moving inland meant I could buy a huge piece of property for a cheap price and build my own vert ramp in the backyard. My girlfriend, Cindy, and another pro skater, Joe Johnson, moved in with me.

While I was in the middle of building my ramps (I decided to put a miniramp right outside my bedroom sliding glass door), I filmed skate parts for the movies *Gleaming the Cube* and *Police Academy 4.* But even out in the boonies, where my nearest neighbor was acres away, my ramp annoyed some people. My neighbor told me that I was going to have to stop skating it and handed me over a list of rules that I was supposed to obey. That was insane! My dad exploded. He had been the mastermind behind the ramp, designing the first wooden bowled corners. He told the neighbor to take a hike and let him know that he wasn't welcome on my property.

Filming at Del Mar in 1983.

Indy air at Del Mar, 1985.

18: FUN AGAIN?

After three months of no contests, I began to itch to compete again. I missed the pressure. Stacy was right—in some way I still needed competition to drive me. I started skating contests again and did what Stacy suggested—I held back in practice and nobody knew what to expect during my contest run. I won; but more important, I was having fun again. I wasn't as worried about how the judges scored me against other skaters. I was skating for fun, and if people thought I lost when I got second place, it didn't bother me anymore.

During the summer of 1988 I went on tour with the Bones Brigade. I had been out of school for two years. Everywhere I looked I could see kids pushing around on skateboards, and Powell was the most popular company at the time. I was making loads of money, which I could never manage to spend (at least, it seemed that way to my twenty-year-old mind). My board was one of the best sellers in the world, and I had a perfect ramp in my backyard. I could skate anytime. I felt like I had accomplished everything I had ever wanted.

The Bones Brigade tour was insane. Thousands of fans showed up at each demo, and the Brigade would have to sign autographs for over three hours straight. Sometimes the police would be called in to control the crowds, and once (I wasn't on the tour at the time) the police had to stop the demo and break up a full-scale riot of hyperactive skaters.

PAPER OR PLASTIC?

After the tour ended, Lance and I traveled to Naples, Italy, for a TV show appearance. Barely anybody we had to work with spoke English, and we didn't speak Italian, so from the start there was little communication. The ramp they'd built for the program was awful. It was so thin that if you bailed, your knees would go through it. One wall beside the ramp was covered with expensive mirrors. I bailed and my board shot off and broke one of them.

But all of that wasn't bad compared with when we were being dressed for the show. The designers brought out a pair of plastic see-through shorts for us to wear. Lance quickly grabbed the blue pair, which were a little darker, but mine were like looking through a window and would have left little to the imagination. I had to go back to the hotel and get a pair of swim trunks to wear underneath. After all of this, they only let us skate for a few minutes before sending us back to the States.

Pointing a melon lien air in my backyard, 1990. This was a cover of Transworld.

My early dream of a bowl connected to a vert ramp was finally realized with the help of my dad in 1990.

19: TROUBLE!

Skating became more popular than anybody ever expected. Part of this was due to the introduction of street skating. Most skaters street skated because it was cheap (you didn't have to pay for a park membership), and also because it was sometimes hard to find a skatepark or a neighborhood ramp to ride on.

I always felt most comfortable on a ramp. I enjoyed street skating and won some street contests, but I had trouble keeping up with all the crazy stuff the top street pros were pulling off. But the new breed of skaters rode both street and vert well. Bucky Lasek, Danny Way, and Colin McKay were a few young kids who brought a whole new style of street-influenced skating to ramps.

I loved the new style of skating; so did the magazines, and they made a big deal out of it. After a while, vert pros with the old, less street-influenced style were being called "dinosaurs." I felt as if I was an old man and couldn't keep up with the kids anymore. I was only in my mid-twenties, but I wondered if I was too old to learn a new style.

Seemingly overnight, the industry began noticing that fewer people were skating. New, smaller companies were starting up, and they had a raw, hardcore image—something the street skaters liked. Powell was seen as an old, out-of-touch company, after having been on top for so many years.

Things were going downhill fast, and then I traveled to Japan and wrecked my knee. I landed a 720 on a demo ramp, squatted too low on my landing, and tore my cartilage. I had to use a wheelchair at the airport, because I couldn't walk.

After taking a week off, my knee felt a little better, but if I bent down it would still lock and shoot pain up and down my leg. I skated a miniramp contest with it tweaked, and then had surgery to repair the cartilage. I felt better after surgery but had to go to physical therapy for two months. I hadn't been off my skateboard for that long since I'd started skating.

Running contests all year long wore my dad out, and he couldn't keep going. In 1989, my parents retired from the NSA, and the skaters threw a party for my dad. He loved it because it showed him they appreciated all that he'd done for skating.

GETTING WORRIED

By 1990 I could tell something was amiss with skating's popularity. Skateboard sales were down and lessening each month. I wasn't too worried, because I never believed that skating could become as unpopular as it had been in the early 1980s.

One day in Los Angeles my girlfriend, Cindy, and I were shopping and saw a cool-looking ring. I bought it and asked her to marry me. She said yes and a few months later we were married in my backyard beside the trampoline and the swimming pool.

Shortly after my wedding I won another NSA vert champion title. I was happy, but in the back of my mind I wondered how I was going to make a good living if skating continued to drop in popularity.

Bad hair and bad acne. You have to be a teenager at some point . . .

20: THE SKY IS FALLING!

It was obvious by 1991 that the skateboarding industry was in trouble. Companies began going out of business, and the few that were left were doing everything possible to cut costs. A year earlier, the Bones Brigade had skated demos in front of thousands of fans; now we'd skate demos and barely a hundred people would show up. There were fewer contests and skaters competing. I won another NSA vert world champion title at the end of the year, but it didn't matter because there weren't enough skaters to notice.

Stacy was burning out on the skateboard industry and told me he was thinking about leaving Powell and Peralta to pursue directing in Hollywood. He would later direct the award-winning movie *Dogtown and Z-Boys.* Stacy revolutionized skate videos and picked a team that's still unsurpassed in contest domination. He felt he didn't have the creative energy to go on with another generation of skaters.

I had been doing a lot of thinking, too. I spoke with another Powell skater, Per Welinder, and we decided to start our own company. If skating was going to die off again, I wanted to be in control of what little bit of it I had left. I called George Powell and Stacy and told them I was leaving. I put all of my money into the new company, which we called Birdhouse. If it failed, I would lose my houses and cars and become almost completely broke. I had confidence in our vision, but I was scared. What would I do if I couldn't skate for a living?

BIRDHOUSE

The first year of Birdhouse sucked. I made just enough money to survive and thought for sure I'd made a mistake. I needed money more than ever, because Cindy was pregnant. I was happy about the fact that I would be a dad, but I became even more worried about my family's future. How would I support them?

Hudson Riley Hawk was born in December 1992. Unfortunately, the movie *Hudson Hawk* came out at around the same time and was a box office bomb. So we called my son by his middle name instead.

I loved skating my backyard ramp, but I had no money to fix it. I had to dodge holes that were rotting into it. I spent a lot of time skating by myself and figured out how to land a varial heelflip lien air, a newer trick similar to ones that skaters like Colin and Danny were doing. I had been trying to land a flip trick for months, so this was a major breakthrough for me. Older skaters with a different style had a difficult time learning flip tricks. To keep progressing, vert skaters had to be able to flip their boards. Like the McTwist, these flip tricks were dividing vert skaters, and I just made it by.

As much as I loved having my own backyard ramp, I couldn't afford two houses. So in 1993, I put the Fallbrook house up for sale, and Cindy, Riley, and I moved into the house I had bought when I was still in high school. Shortly after that I organized another Birdhouse Summer Tour. Birdhouse was barely making money, so I had to cut costs and use my own minivan to travel. It was too small, but we jammed five skaters with all their pads and clothes in it and drove around the country for one month straight. A lot of times skate shops refused to pay us for demos (our fee was $400 to cover expenses), even though they said they would. By the time we drove back to California, Birdhouse had lost thousands of dollars on the tour just paying for gas and other expenses on the road.

What, me a computer freak? Back in 1993 I tried to supplement my income by editing videos.

21: A NEW LOW

The following year was even worse than 1993. Per and I had a meeting to discuss dumping Birdhouse. It wasn't making money, and we figured we were destined to lose everything we'd invested in the company. But we decided to give it one more year. We had nothing better to fall back on.

Vert was almost extinct. There were barely any skate contests. The few that took place were poorly run and the checks usually bounced. Skaters lost money going to contests because they had to cover their own expenses. Skate companies were reluctant to sponsor NSA events, so the new organizers spent all the association's savings and it went out of business.

Per and I stopped making my pro model, since it wasn't selling anyway, and I retired from skating competitions. Or, more accurately, because there was no demand, I was laid off.

At home, things unfortunately weren't much better. Cindy and

I realized that even though we were good friends, we weren't working as husband and wife. We agreed to get divorced, and we are closer now than when we were married. We live a few miles from each other and, I'm proud to say, have always kept Riley as our top priority.

SNOOPY HELPS FIND A DATE

In 1994, a request for a skateboarding demo was a rare thing, but Charles M. Schulz, the creator of the *Peanuts* comic strip, organized a demo with skaters, bikers, and Rollerbladers. On my flight to Santa Rosa, where the demo took place, was a cute blonde named Erin, who was in the show. We started talking and got along well. I was also blown away by how natural she was with Riley. They painted together and played for hours. After the demo we started dating.

Riley is either smelling something bad (my pads?)
or trying not to laugh at my hair, 2000.

My dad, who died in 1995. He's the one person I wish
could see how far everything has come.

22: CANCER STINKS

By 1995 I was convinced that my involvement in the skateboarding industry was coming to an end. Skating was on the upswing, but it was a very slow process. I wasn't sure if Birdhouse could last another year without a big jump in sales. But as much of a bummer as 1994 was (except for meeting Erin), the following year was like riding an out-of-control roller coaster. One month I would be up, happier than I thought possible; the next I'd be more depressed than I had been in years.

My dad had a nagging cough that wouldn't go away. After many visits with the doctor, he was diagnosed with lung cancer and was told he had less than a year to live. He had flown airplanes through World War II and the Korean War, waved off a heart attack like it was an annoying gnat, and outworked skaters who were a third his age when building a ramp, and was now getting weaker by the day. Many of the skaters he had known during the previous ten years started visiting or sending cards when they heard the news. It meant a lot to my family to have that show of support. And it validated everything my dad had done for skating, even if he could be hardheaded sometimes.

EXTREME GAMES

At the start of the year there was a rumor that ESPN was organizing an event that would be like the Olympics, but for cutting-edge activities like BMX, skateboarding, rock climbing, and a bunch of other alternative sports. They were holding it in Rhode Island and calling it the Extreme Games, a truly horrible name. Skaters didn't know if the event was a positive or negative thing for skateboarding. In the movies, skateboarding had always been treated like a pastime for rebels, so skaters were suspicious as to how a TV network would handle it.

I skated in the games and won the vert contest. While I was there, my dad was in the hospital, so before a run, when the camera filmed me, I looked into it and said, "Hi, Dad." I knew he'd get a kick out of that, because nobody bragged about me as much as my dad. I was surprised at how many people recognized me after the contest aired on TV, but, more important, I was excited that skating had been seen by millions of people around the world.

WORST TOUR EVER

I was planning on canceling the upcoming Birdhouse summer tour to stay home with my dad, but he wouldn't let me. "What? Do you think I'm going to die in a month?" he asked me.

I called him every night from the road, and during these conversations I let him know how much he meant to me. I wanted him to know that I appreciated all the effort he'd put into making sure I was happy. He'd crack jokes, but I could tell he knew what I meant.

I was skating Woodward Camp as part of a series of demos in Pennsylvania when I got a message that I had an urgent phone call. It was my mom telling me that Dad had died the night before. I didn't know what to do. I didn't start crying. There were crowds of skaters asking for autographs, but I just walked off the street course and into the woods to grieve in private. I wanted to be alone to think about what my dad had meant to me, and how much I'd miss him. It still blows me away to think of how much he did for me. I flew home that afternoon.

We had a wake at my sister Lenore's house. People who had been involved in skating over the previous twenty years came over and exchanged affectionate stories about my dad grumbling and complaining around skate contests, but loving it at the same time. Skaters who were troublemakers told me that my dad's influence helped change their lives for the better. I knew that would have pleased my dad and meant more to him than anything else he'd done for skating.

My dad fixing my private ramp in 1989.

23: MORE CHANGES

In 1995 skating was finally making enough of a comeback that I could relax for the first time in years. My board was rereleased and was selling well, and with the help of other popular skaters on the Birdhouse team, the company actually began making money.

Even though it was expensive, I convinced Per that we needed to build a private ramp for the team. I found a massive warehouse in Irvine, which is between San Diego and Los Angeles, and had a ramp built. It wasn't as close as a backyard ramp—it took me more than an hour to drive there—but at least it was a private ramp, where I could skate anytime.

There were other things I wanted to do now that I was making a decent income. I asked Erin to marry me on the empty lot where we planned to have a new house built. She said yes.

While Erin made wedding plans, I skated in contests around the United States. I slammed hard at a contest in Seal Beach and sprained my ankle worse than I ever had before. But I couldn't take the time off to let it heal, because the Birdhouse Tour was scheduled to start in a couple of weeks. I used an expensive ankle brace, which had springs and metal bars in it to support my ankle, and skated anyway. Two weeks into the tour I sprained my other ankle just as badly. The first one still hadn't healed. It hurt to walk, and my ankles puffed up like marshmallows and turned a dark shade of purple.

I took pain medicine and iced my ankles whenever I wasn't skating. But after a week of constant pain, I was feeling awful. I didn't want to let any fans down, so I kept going. After six weeks of skating with ankle pain, I was totally stressed out. I was in my late twenties and somebody or something was telling me that I was too old for this. I debated for the last week of the tour whether I should step back and just skate whenever I felt like it, instead of filling my life up with demos and contests.

Smith grind during the grind of a summer tour in Atlanta, 2000.

I took a few weeks off from skating after the tour ended. It was the end of summer, and the break relieved some of the pressures of touring. Erin and I were married that September and had a honeymoon in Hawaii, which gave me more time to repair. I felt good. I had a wife, a son, and a private ramp. After years of an uncertain lifestyle, I finally felt secure.

MADE-FOR-TV DRAMA

By 1997, the third year of the X Games (they changed their name—good move), things took a weird twist. ESPN was reporting a rivalry between Andy Macdonald and me (we had each won an earlier X Games). This couldn't have been further from the truth, because Andy and I were good friends. We even skated together in doubles events. But to the millions of people watching TV, it looked like we were two gunslingers about to shoot it out on the X Games vert ramp. Both Andy and I were upset about it, and in every interview we did we explained that skating wasn't a sport where you had to beat somebody else. It was about having fun and outperforming yourself.

My second run of the finals was my best run in a long time, and I decided I couldn't do any better. I started to try 900s for the rest of my ramp time. (I had been trying to land a 9 for more than a decade but took a break when I broke a rib.) I didn't come close to landing one that year, but at least I was trying.

I won the contest but was bummed with all the reporters who asked me about "my perfect run," as an ESPN commentator called it. I've had many contest runs that I thought were better. Now it's known as a legendary run because some ESPN announcer made an exaggerated comment.

That year Birdhouse did really well, and we could afford to rent an RV when we toured. We could actually lie down and sleep. No more stinky, cheap vans packed with skaters. Erin, Riley, and I moved into our new home. It was a good thing, too, because we were about to have an addition to the Hawk family.

At eighteen feet, this was the tallest ramp built for skating. It allowed us to go higher than ever before. Las Vegas, 1999.

24: THE END

Inspired by Stacy Peralta, I had always wanted to make a skate-board video that would be watched for years to come. Most videos at the time were shot with digital cameras, but we started shooting *The End* in 1998 with film, which is much more expensive and complicated to shoot with. By the time we were finished, the video cost about ten times what it cost to produce the average skate video. But it was worth it.

One of the reasons we called it *The End* was that I figured it would be the last time I'd put a lot of effort into my video part. I figured by age thirty (I was twenty-nine at the time) I wasn't going to be able to withstand the abuse I had when I was younger. No pro skater had been successfully competitive past thirty.

Every skater on Birdhouse was in charge of his own part and was given the freedom to create a theme. Jeremy Klein and Heath

Kirchart hired a stuntman to roll a fiery van and skated around explosions and fire. Andrew Reynolds hired an orangutan. I built a dream ramp with a loop in a Mexican bullring.

I had always wanted to ride through a loop, inspired by the Hot Wheels track I had played with as a kid. I didn't know of anybody else ever landing it. I had tried it once before for an ad but lost control when I'd exited the loop, and wiped out onto my back. Back then, I had designed the loop poorly. For the video, I figured out how to build one that would make it easier to complete. Also, a huge ramp connected to the loop was built to make landing a 900 easier. Landing the loop and a 900 were two of my main goals for the video.

Throughout my skating career I have had certain tricks I wanted to land. Thanks to persistence and practice, I have crossed them all off the list. When I landed the loop (with only a few slams and one compressed vertebra), I only had one left—the 900. I was scared. What if I slammed on my head or broke a bone? I'd be stuck going to a sketchy hospital in Tijuana.

I dropped in, the cameras rolled, and . . . I couldn't make myself commit to landing. I'd spin and spin and bail, get up and repeat the process. I was disgusted with myself. I took off my helmet and shook my head. The cameras all clicked off, and nobody said anything. I knew I'd let people down, but what really hurt was that I'd let myself down. I wanted to crawl into a hole and hide.

As bummed as I was about failing to land the 9, the pain was lessened by what Erin had told me a few days before—she was pregnant. We were so happy, and Riley was excited because he wanted a little brother to play with. Shortly after *The End* premiered, my son Spencer was born.

I'm glad *The End* was loved by skaters. I'm proud of the movie, even though it reminds me of not landing the 9; but many people still tell me that it's their favorite skate video.

Can't I even sneeze in private? There is no time to be sick while on tour, so you just gotta go with it. Gigantic Skatepark Tour, 2000.

A backside nosegrind over the death box rail in Encinitas, 1998.

25: 1999, THE YEAR OF THE 9

I didn't tell anybody, but I knew in January 1999 that at the end of the year I would stop skating in contests. The decision was different from the other times I had flirted with competitive retirement. It wasn't due to any crushing pressures that I felt; it was the sense that I was satisfied with what I had accomplished. I didn't want to follow the rigorous competition schedule anymore, and I didn't feel the burning desire to skate my best in a contest. After fifteen years of pro contests, I wanted to return to the days when I just skated with my friends. I still pushed myself, but I knew I could go in any direction I wanted and not have to worry about people judging me.

Perhaps I should have "retired" at the start of the year, because once I'd made the decision to stop, it was almost impossible to make myself excited about a contest. But it was still a fun year. Disney made the movie *Tarzan,* and the artists told me that they'd used footage of me from *The End* to get ideas for Tarzan's movements through the trees. This was a huge honor and scored me some serious bonus points with Riley, because he was a big Disney fan. My fame from skating meant nothing to him, but being involved in a Disney movie—now I was cool. He and I filmed a commercial for the movie's video release.

MY LAST X GAMES

I had to drag myself to the X Games that year, which I wasn't too excited about. I didn't skate my best during the vert contest, but I looked forward to one of my favorite events—best trick. This was a loose format where I could skate with five friends. We'd do our best to impress one another. When the contest started, I wanted to land a varial 720. I hadn't even thought about doing a 900. I hadn't tried it in a long time.

I landed the varial 720 in the first fifteen minutes of the event and had fifteen minutes left to skate. I didn't have anything else planned. I thought it would take me the entire time to land the varial 720. I walked up the ramp, thinking of tricks to try, but once I put the tail of my board on the coping I knew I wanted to spin a few 9s. Not because I was sure I could do it, but to stoke out the crowd.

I had been attempting 900s for more than ten years. I remembered the last time I'd thought I was close to landing one. I ended up slamming into the ramp, fracturing a rib. Another time before that I got lost in the middle of my spin, landed on top of the ramp, and bounced off onto the flatbottom. There were parts of the trick, such as how to control the spin and adjust my weight for the landing, that I just didn't know how to do. Once I would solve one problem, another would present itself. I had my doubts that it was even possible to land one.

My first one felt good! This was odd, because usually I was more scared and had trouble controlling the spin. As I kneeslid down the X Games ramp from my first attempt, I thought that I might be able to come closer than I ever had before. I tried a few more. Each time I felt more comfortable. I usually had problems spotting the ramp and seeing where I was about to land because I was spinning so fast, but now I had control of the spin. Every time I bailed, I became more focused. The cheering crowd, the announcer, and the music all faded into nothing. I didn't even think about landing it; I was concentrating on making adjustments to correct my spin. Every try would bring me closer and provide one more hint to what I was doing wrong.

On my twelfth try I felt an odd sensation; it was the impact of my wheels hitting the ramp and my hand skimming the ramp surface. I was trying to keep my balance and squatted so that my center of gravity was more stable. I began kickturning on the other side of the ramp before I realized that I had just landed the 9.

My fist shot up automatically, and I yelled as loud as I could. All the skaters ran on the ramp and tackled me before picking me up and carrying me around. It was the happiest moment of my skate career.

To my surprise, newspapers and news programs from all over the world reported my landing the 900 as a major sporting event. Skateboarding had never received coverage that widespread before. It shocked me and made me feel a little weird. A few years earlier I was being harassed for being a skater, and now I was being celebrated for landing a new trick.

The 900.

26: THE GOOD LIFE

After the '99 X Games I skated in a few more contests and won the last one of the year. After my last run I told Grant Brittain, the old manager at Del Mar who is now a world-famous skate photographer, that it was my last vert contest run. He nodded and smiled at me. It was cool that the guy who had signed my slips for Skateboard PE back when it was considered a loser activity was there when I stopped competing. I still skate specialty events, like doubles and best trick, but only because those are relaxed and more of a novelty.

CRAZIER THAN EVER

I thought my life would be less busy once I quit contests, but the opposite happened. Activision came out with a *Tony Hawk's*

Pro Skater video game, which became the best selling video game in the world at the time of its release. The game added to the 900 media frenzy and made me more popular than ever. Any spare time was quickly booked with demos and appearances.

One of my dreams always had been to show the world what skateboarding was really like. I was tired of television shows always presenting skating in a competitive way, so I started working as an ESPN commentator. I didn't like that people thought skaters were rebellious clowns, so I started 900 Films, a production company, with two of my friends and worked with ESPN to create a TV program called *Tony Hawk's Gigantic Skatepark Tour*. We had control over how the show looked. I gathered a bunch of my friends and fellow pros, and we toured around the world skating the best skateparks we could find. We showed parents and kids that skateboarding is a positive influence and that competition is only a small part of the picture. One of the things I'm most proud of is that many people tell me that *Tony Hawk's Gigantic Skatepark Tour* is fun to watch. They say it made them appreciate the dedication it takes to become a good skater.

Erin and I had another baby boy, Keegan, in 2001. Riley enjoys skating and always goes on tour with me if it doesn't get in the way of school. Spencer, who just turned three, is a daredevil, and I'm a bit afraid of what might happen if and when he gets near a skateboard. Activision released two other versions of my game and each one sold better than the last. (The best part of having your own video game is that you can play games and tell your wife that you are working.)

I never expected to make a career out of skateboarding. I think I lasted so long as a professional because I was always thankful for what skateboarding did for me. I enjoyed skating with my buddies and pushing myself to learn new tricks. The fame that came with it never interfered with my skating. Skating taught me self-discipline at a young age and helped channel my frustrations and turn them into something useful. Even if I hadn't been successful at it—if I'd never made a dime—I would still be pushing around with my kids at the local skatepark. I don't know anything that's as fun as skateboarding, or any activity that could have better shaped my life.

Riley, when he was eight years old, doing a backside 180 in Tokyo. I hadn't even stepped on a skateboard when I was eight.

I built this ramp so we could cut away pieces to make the gap larger and larger. Me 540-ing the eighteen-foot divide, 2000.

Backside overturn grind over the death box rail at Encinitas in 1999.

Ten Favorite CDs

The Clash: *London Calling*
Beatles: *Sgt. Pepper's Lonely Hearts Club Band*
Kraftwerk: *Electric Cafe*
Jane's Addiction: *Nothing's Shocking*
AC/DC: *Back in Black*
Pixies: *Doolittle*
Radiohead: *OK Computer*
Ministry: *A Mind Is a Terrible Thing to Taste*
U2: *Joshua Tree*
Beastie Boys: *Ill Communication*

Ten Favorite Tricks

540—I can do many variations, and it's always a crowd pleaser.
Backside ollie—It is the one ollie on vert that I feel like I have total
     control over.

720—I learned it in 1985 and it still feels good to land a clean one.

Caballerial—Steve Caballero, what more can you say?

Elguerial—Eddie Elguera. Ditto.

Backside lipslide—It is one of the scariest tricks to learn, and they don't feel that hard anymore.

Tailslide—It can be done with almost any amount of speed. A good filler trick.

Tailgrab—It always looks stylish.

360 flip—I practiced it every day for months before finally figuring it out. One of the few (street) flip tricks I can do consistently.

Varial—The first trick I ever made up (backside). I just can't let it go.

Ten Favorite Movies

Fast Times at Ridgemont High

Repo Man

Robocop

The Usual Suspects

Reservoir Dogs

Being John Malkovich

Living in Oblivion

Happy Gilmore

Airplane!

Prince of Darkness

Ten Hardest Tricks to Learn

900—It took me five years just to get the guts to try it, and then another five years of failed attempts.

Kickflip McTwist—I tried it (and it only) for nearly two months before finally making one.

540—Learning to spin is only half the battle.

Kickflip—It just seems impossible when you first try it.

Frontside invert—I could only do Miller flips at first. I still miss the coping half the time.

Stalefish 540—Grabbing this way slows down your spin.

Ollie 540—I didn't really think it was possible until I tried it lower.

Ollie blunt—It's like relearning an ollie.

Backside revert—You can't see as you turn, and it has great whiplash potential.

Ho-ho—I could never do one properly. It takes a background in gymnastics.

Ten Favorite Types of Food

Japanese—unagi and zaru soba

Indian—chicken korma

Thai—gaeng mussaman kai

Italian—spaghetti and meatballs

Jamaican—jerk chicken

Greek—hummus and gyros

Pizza—pepperoni or pesto and chicken

In N Out—the #1, no onions

Taco Bell—bean and cheese burrito, no onions

Erin's cooking—chicken katsu

Ten Favorite Skaters

Eddie Elguera

Steve Caballero

Mark Gonzales

Christian Hosoi

Bob Burnquist

Bucky Lasek

Danny Way

Colin McKay

Eric Koston

Rick McCrank

Favorite Contest Run

Munster World Cup, 1998. I made every trick I had hoped to, and threw in a couple I wasn't sure about. My contest performances that year were not outstanding up until that point. I couldn't improve on my second run in the finals, so I did an entire old-school routine for my last run.

Tony's Ten Website Links

Birdhouse: www.birdhouseskateboards.com

Quiksilver: www.quiksilver.com

Hawk Clothing: www.hawkclothing.com

Hawk Shoes: www.hawkshoes.com

Arnette: www.arnette.com

TSG: www.tsgprotection.com

Ramp Logic: www.ramplogic.com

Fan club: www.clubtonyhawk.com

The Tony Hawk Foundation: www.tonyhawkfoundation.org

Activision: www.activision02.com

Mom and me.

ACKNOWLEDGMENTS

Erin, Riley, Spencer, and Keegan; Mom and Eric; Lenore, Dick, Greg, and John; Pat, Alan, Hagen, and Emily; Steve, Pamm, Will, and Cameron. All at THI, SHP, WMA, Slam, Blitz, 900, Hawk, Quik, Atlas, Activision, Neversoft, BSP, Rebel Waltz, TWS, Big Brother, Slap, ESPN, Redline, Heinz, TSG, Arnette, Mainframe, Nixon, and Apple; and all my friends who will hopefully forgive me for not listing them.

Another day, another demo. Frontside stiffy in Atlanta while on the Gigantic Skatepark Tour, 2000.

Combining tricks is one of the funnest aspects of skating. A varial 540 on the Gigantic Skatepark Tour, 2000.

PHOTO CREDITS

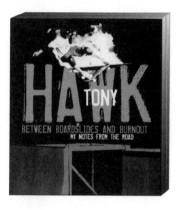